The Will of God Workbook

by
R. S. "Bud" Miller, D.D.
Publisher
Betty Miller, D.M.
Author
www.BibleResources.org

Overcoming Life Series

Christ Unlimited — P.O. Box 850 — Dewey, AZ 86327   USA

Unless otherwise indicated, all Scripture quotations are taken from the King James Version of the Holy Bible (KJV).

Overcoming Life Series:

The Will of God Workbook

ISBN 1-57149-005-1

Copyright (c) 1995-2013

R. S. "Bud" and Betty Miller

P. O. Box 850

Dewey, Arizona 86327

Published by

Christ Unlimited Publishing

P. O. Box 850

Dewey, Arizona 86327

Publisher: Pastor R. S. "Bud" Miller

Printed in the United States of America.

All rights reserved under International Copyright Law. Contents and/or cover may not be reproduced in whole or in part in any form without the express written consent of the Publisher.

Christ Unlimited — P.O. Box 850 — Dewey, AZ 86327   USA

Contents

Personal Introduction

A lack of education will not hinder anyone from taking this course, and a doctor's degree will not help. However, one requirement that is necessary for this course to benefit the student is a total commitment to God. The Holy Spirit is our teacher, and we can learn if we come to God as little children. Being hungry to know God is a necessary prerequisite in order for this course to be of help.

If any of us are to receive truth, we must seek God, who is truth, with our whole hearts. We must seek Jesus first, then the knowledge of His Word will be revealed to us. Therefore, I want to emphasize once again the need to become as "a little child" in our approach to learning God's Word (Matt. 18:1-4; Jer. 29:13).

We need to come humbly before God, asking Him to remove any "know-it-all" attitudes, in order to be teachable. By laying down everything we thought we knew, we give God a chance to correct things we have believed that were wrong. Then we can begin to live the overcoming lives that God intended for His children to experience.

This course is part of a larger course based on the Overcoming Life Series, nine books taken from our first published book, How To Overcome Through the Christ Unlimited. That book, given to us under the anointing of the Holy Spirit, covers most of the basic things a Christian needs to know to get started on a victorious, overcoming walk with the Lord.

Christ Unlimited — P.O. Box 850 — Dewey, AZ 86327   USA

We have purposely kept this course simple for the average Christian who needs help in understanding how to study the Word and how to sort out principles and concepts when he, or she, reads the Bible; however, it also is for the seminary student. In addition, it is designed for students who desire to use it as a correspondence course. They can learn from it, even if they are totally alone and without a human teacher. The Holy Spirit always is there to teach us as we study about His Word.

On the other hand, groups with a teacher, or moderator, also can use this course to advantage. Our prayer is that however this course is taken, each student will complete it a different person and be conformed more into the image of Christ our Lord.

Bud and Betty Miller

Christ Unlimited — P.O. Box 850 — Dewey, AZ 86327   USA

The Will of God Workbook

Section One

"God's Word Is His Will"

Christ Unlimited — P.O. Box 850 — Dewey, AZ 86327   USA

The Will of God Workbook
Section One: "God's Word Is His Will"
Expository Introduction

[Author's Note: This workbook is the third in the Overcoming Life Series, which includes nine books and workbooks. Lessons also have supplementary material. Answers are provided at the end of the workbook and do not have to be the exact wording in many cases. The student simply needs to make sure that he, or she, has caught the concept or principle from the Word of God.]

Believers need to understand more about knowing the will of God. Very simply: God's Word is His will. We know this is true, because the Bible tells us so.

In the beginning was the Word, and the Word was with God, and the Word was God. The same was in the beginning with God. All things were made by him; and without him was not any thing made that was made . . . He was in the world, and the world was made by him, and the world knew him not.

John 1:1-3,10

The Bible is the revealed Word of God, although it was given to us through more than 40 human authors. Actually, the Bible is referred to as "the last will and testament" of Jesus. Bible is simply an English transliteration of the Greek word for "book," which is byblos. So the Word of God is the Book by which we should be living.

Christ Unlimited — P.O. Box 850 — Dewey, AZ 86327   USA

The Apostle Paul wrote to Timothy:

All scripture is given by inspiration of God, and is profitable for doctrine, for reproof, for correction, for instruction in righteousness: that the man of God may be perfect, thoroughly furnished unto all good works.

2 Timothy 3:16,17

When Jesus died on the cross, His "last will and testament" to us went into effect (Heb. 9:16-18). God wants us to receive our inheritance according to His will as it is set forth in the Bible (Gal. 3:7-29).

Two Greek words are translated <u>Word</u> in the Bible, when referring to God's Word or to Jesus: <u>logos</u> and <u>rhema</u>.[1]

According to <u>Vine's Dictionary</u>, there are two main meanings of <u>logos</u>. The first is "the expression of thought" (a conception or idea), "a saying or statement," or a discourse, speech, or instruction <u>by God</u> or by <u>Christ</u>. Vine wrote:

The phrase, "the Word of the Lord," is the revealed will of God (very frequent in the Old Testament) and used as a direct revelation given by Christ...it is the message from the Lord, delivered with His authority and made effective by His power ...sometimes it is used as the sum of God's utterances.

The second major meaning of <u>logos</u>, according to <u>Vine's</u>, is:

The Personal Word, a title of the Son of God...His distinct and superfinite Personality, His relation in the "Godhead" (not pertaining to the mere companionhship of Deity but to "the most intimate communion") and to "His Deity," "His incarnation," and "the reality and totality of His human nature <u>and</u> His glory."

<u>Rhema</u> denotes the Word of God which is spoken, according to Vine, who added:

> The significance of <u>rhema</u> (as distinct from <u>logos</u>) is exemplified in the injunction to take "the sword of the Spirit," which is the word of God, (Eph. 6:17); here the reference is not to the whole Bible as such, but to the individual scripture which the Spirit brings to our remembrance for us in time of need, the prerequisite being the regular storing of the mind with Scripture.

To summarize these definitions, usually we simply say that the <u>logos</u> is the written Word of God and the living Word, Jesus. <u>Rhema</u> is a Spirit-breathed Word brought to our minds in times of need. When we read the Bible, and suddenly, a word, a phrase, or a verse seems to "come alive" to us, we have experienced or received a <u>rhema</u> from God through the Holy Spirit.

Sometimes <u>rhema</u> words are given us through prophecy, and the key proof that any spoken "word" is indeed from God is <u>if it agrees with the written Word</u> already given. Generally speaking, we should order our lives according to the will of God revealed in the

Bible and seldom by words of prophecies. Prophetic words should usually be words of confirmation to us.

Seeking the Will of God

Some Christians seek "prophets" to give them words from God when they should first search the scriptures for an answer. There are many "self-styled prophets" out there today, and Christians should be very careful to test all things by the written Word of God (1 Thess. 5:21; 1 John 4:1). But what if the answer is not in the Word of God?

In general terms or in principle, our answers are always to be found in the Bible; however, specific details that depend on one's culture, society, or circumstances will not be in the Bible. For example, the Bible tells us we can and should expect through faith to have our needs met, so if we need transportation, we can believe God for that. However, the Bible does not tell us whether to buy a car, a truck, a van, or a bicycle. Nor does it tell us what make, model, or color is the right one. We must find the one that will be what God knows is best for us which is appropriating His wisdom, which will be His will for us.

Of course, the best way is to seek the face of the Lord for an answer, which we may receive through an "inner witness" that amounts to a "knowing" or to peace in our spirits (James 3:17). Some Christians, however, are not yet spiritually mature enough, or close enough to the Holy Spirit, to discern God's will in this way. So they seek other ways.

Christ Unlimited — P.O. Box 850 — Dewey, AZ 86327   USA

One of those ways through which Christians try to find the will of God, when His will in a certain situation is not spelled out in the Bible, is to ask God for a sign. Sometimes opening the Bible and asking God to speak to them through a certain verse can be seeking a sign.

It is not wrong to seek God by looking to His Word in this way; however, if this is the only means through which one seeks Him, it can open the door for deception. Other things must accompany searching the Word, such as having a committed life and a willingness to obey the commandments of God at any cost.

Two other methods of asking for signs are through "fleeces" and through "open" or "closed" doors.

Basically, we do not advise seeking answers through signs from God of any kind.

Seeking signs also is known as "tempting God." In **Luke 4:9-12**, when Jesus was being tempted of the devil, the enemy sought to get Jesus to show the people He was the Son of God by performing a supernatural sign. That sign was to be a showing of God's supernatural protection of Jesus if He leaped from the pinnacle of the temple.

A "fleece" basically is asking God to give you a sign in a supernatural way, while asking for "open or closed doors" simply is asking God to use circumstances as a sign. People base this on **Revelation 3:8**, where Jesus is called the One Who opens and closes doors. But the Bible does not tell us to ask for this as a "sign."

Many times, Christians confuse the two and talk about "fleeces" when they really mean asking God to operate through circumstances. Since the Day of Pentecost, Christians have had the Holy Spirit within them as Counselor, and asking God for supernatural signs can open the door to great deceit by the enemy.

Under the Old Covenant, the Holy Spirit did not indwell men, so God did more outwardly supernatural things. The term "fleece" comes from the story of Gideon, found in **Judges 6-8**. An Israelite of the tribe of Manasseh, Gideon was called to lead Israel. Being an humble man from a poor family, he was fearful and had no confidence.

When the angel of the Lord appeared to him and called him to lead Israel into battle against the Midianites, Gideon asked for a sign, which actually became two signs (**Judg. 6:36-40**). He first asked that a certain fleece (sheep's skin) laid out on the ground would be wet with dew in the morning, while the ground all around it was dry. God made that happen to the extent that a bowl full of water was wrung out of the fleece. But then Gideon asked for another sign. He asked for the reverse to happen, for the fleece to be dry while the ground around it was wet with dew. And the Lord also did that.

Notice, however, that even Gideon was concerned as he asked for a sign. In **Judges 6:39**, he approached God in prayer not to be angry with him for asking thusly. The Lord already had told him he was not only to fight this battle, but that he was to win it (v. 14).

In Christian circles today, asking God for a sign that something is really from Him is often referred to as a "fleece." However, unless it involves asking for something supernatural to happen, it usually amounts to asking God to use circumstances as a sign to show you His will. Not many Christians would ask for a real fleece, a supernatural sign.

Our Guides Are the Bible and the Holy Spirit

God may honor a new ("baby") Christian's request for a sign because that person may not yet know how to find the will of God. However, guidance on "fleeces" or circumstances can lead us into error, because the devil also can open or close doors or bring about the requested circumstances.

An example would be for a Christian to pray and ask God to send a red car by his house if it was God's will for him to witness to his neighbor. The devil could restrain any cars from coming by the house, and that person then would believe he was not to witness to his neighbor. Also, since the Bible already tells us God's will in regard to witnessing, I find it very unlikely that God would send a red car by that house!

The Bible tells us in **Mark 16:15** that Jesus said for His followers to:

...Go ye into all the world, and preach the gospel to every creature."

The devil cannot hinder or tamper with guidance by changing what is written in the Bible. **John 16:13** says that the Holy Spirit will

Christ Unlimited — P.O. Box 850 — Dewey, AZ 86327   USA

guide us into all truth and show us things to come. We should be guided by the written Word and the Holy Spirit. There is a basic pattern in God's Word for such questions as:

"Should I move to another city?"

"Is he, or she, the right mate for me?

"Should I go into full-time ministry?"

Let's look at Romans 12:1-3:

I beseech you therefore, brethren, by the mercies of God, that ye present your bodies a living sacrifice, holy, acceptable unto God, which is your reasonable service. And be not conformed to this world; but be ye transformed by the renewing of your mind, that ye may prove what is that good, and acceptable, and perfect, will of God. For I say, through the grace given unto me, to every man that is among you, not to think of himself more highly than he ought to think; but to think soberly according as God hath dealt to every man the measure of faith.

According to those verses we need to take the following steps to arrive at our answers:

1. We must present ourselves as living sacrifices; in other words, be totally committed to God. Luke 14:26-33 tells us that dying to self-will and living in the will of God is "bearing our crosses."

2. We must renew our minds from the world's thinking to be conformed to the Word of God. If we renew our minds to God's Word, we will "delight in doing His will" (Ps. 40:8). We will not delight in His will until He does an extensive work within us so that our

carnal minds are renewed from worldly ways. This is why we must give first place to the Lord and His Word in our lives: to have the mind of Christ (1 Cor. 2:14-16).

3. We must "prove" or "test" our decisions by the Word in order to know His perfect will (1 John 4:1).

4. We must approach Him with humility. Spiritual pride has been, and still is, the downfall of many. Pride and trust in one's own knowledge of God's Word instead of childlike trust in God is "faith in one's own faith" instead of faith in God. The psalmist David called pride "the great transgression" (Ps. 19:11-14).

5. We must seek God's will with "a sober mind." Logic is not sinful. Only the carnal mind — the mind attuned to worldly or fleshly thinking — is opposite to God's thinking (Rom. 8:7). When we receive God's will on any given subject, if we have truly committed it to the Lord and are willing to obey Him, we will find our minds in agreement with God's direction.

6. We must believe <u>in faith</u> that God will reveal His will to us (James 1:6). Knowing the will of God is not an automatic thing. It takes <u>trust, obedience, study, prayer, and seeking</u>, as well as a total commitment. The six keys or steps listed above are simply guidelines to seek the will of God given us by the Apostle Paul. There are no "seven steps to victory," no formulas. Knowing God's will is a matter of relationship, not striving.

Only a daily walk with God, fellowshipping with Him, will cause us to understand His will and bring us victory in our lives.

Christ Unlimited — P.O. Box 850 — Dewey, AZ 86327   USA

Endnotes

[1]Vine, W. E. <u>Vine's Expository Dictionary of Old and New Testament Words</u>, (Old Tappan: Fleming H. Revell Company, 1981), Vol. 4, pp. 229,230.

Lesson for Section One

[Author's Note: All Scripture references that answer these questions have been given. Please do not look at the answer page until you have answered the questions in your own words. This is not a test, but an expository lesson to help you learn.]

I. Defining God's Will

A. Define God's will

_____

In the beginning was the Word, and the Word was with God, and the Word was God.

John 1:1

B. The two Greek words used for the Word of God are: (See Expository Introduction.)

_____ and _____

1. Essentially, what does each word mean?

a. _____

b. _____

Christ Unlimited — P.O. Box 850 — Dewey, AZ 86327   USA

2. Should these "words" agree?

_____

3. Can they disagree and yet both be right?

_____

4. The word _____ also is used in Scripture as a synonym for Jesus Christ, the Living Word.
   Reference: John 1:1

II. How To Find God's Will

A. There are two avenues for finding God's will in a certain matter or situation. What are they?

1. _____

2. _____

Howbeit when he, the Spirit of truth, is come, he will guide you into all truth: for he shall not speak of himself; but whatsoever he shall hear, that shall he speak: and he will shew you things to come.

John 16:13

Christ Unlimited — P.O. Box 850 — Dewey, AZ 86327   USA

All scripture is given by inspiration of God, and is profitable for doctrine, for reproof, for correction, for instruction in righteousness: That the man of God may be perfect, thoroughly furnished unto all good works.

2 Timothy 3:16,17

B. If we ask anything according to God's will, are we assured of the answer?

_____

And this is the confidence that we have in him, that, if we ask anything according to his will, he heareth us: And if we know that he hear us, whatsoever we ask, we know that we have the petitions that we desired of him.

1 John 5:14,15

C. What are two common ways in which Christians seek at times to find the will of God through signs?

1. _____

2. _____

   a. Who in the Bible "put out a fleece?"

_____

Reference: Judges 6:36-40

Christ Unlimited — P.O. Box 850 — Dewey, AZ 86327   USA

b. What is a "fleece?"

_____

D. Why can seeking signs open a person up to error?

_____

Reference: 2 Corinthians 11:13,14

III. Guidelines Given in the Bible

A. The Apostle Paul gave at least six guidelines by which Christians can find the Lord's will in personal situations. List the six.

1. _____

2. _____

3. _____

4. _____

5. _____

6. _____

Reference: Romans 12:1-3; 1 Corinthians 1:21-25; 2:14-16

Christ Unlimited — P.O. Box 850 — Dewey, AZ 86327   USA

a. What does "bearing our crosses" mean?

_____

If any man come to me, and hate not his father, and mother, and wife, and children, and brethren, and sisters, yea, and his own life also, he cannot be my disciple. And whosoever doth not bear his cross, and come after me, cannot be my disciple.

Luke 14:26,27

b. Who cannot be Jesus' disciple?

_____

B. Is knowing God's will an automatic thing for Christians?

_____

1. What are some of the things it takes to get to the point of hearing God?

_____

_____

_____

Christ Unlimited — P.O. Box 850 — Dewey, AZ 86327   USA

2. Jeremiah gave us a clue as to how we can find God or
   His will. What is it?

   _____

For I know the thoughts that I think toward you, saith the Lord,
thoughts of peace, and not of evil, to give you an expected end.
Then shall ye call upon me, and ye shall go and pray unto me,
and I will hearken unto you. And ye shall seek me, and find me,
when you search for me with all your heart.

Jeremiah 29:11-13

3. What is the "great transgression?"

   _____

Moreover by them (God's words) is thy servant warned: and in
keeping of them there is great reward. Who can understand his
errors? cleanse thou me from secret faults. Keep back thy
servant also from presumptuous sins; let them not have
dominion over me: then shall I be upright, and I shall be
innocent from the great transgression.

Psalm 19:11-14

Other References: Psalm 119:21; Proverbs 16:18

Christ Unlimited — P.O. Box 850 — Dewey, AZ 86327   USA

4. When do we <u>delight</u> in doing the Lord's will?

_____

_____

But the natural man receiveth not the things of the Spirit of God: for they are foolishness unto him: neither can he know them, because they are spiritually discerned. But he that is spiritual judgeth all things, yet he himself is judged of no man. For who hath known the mind of the Lord, that he may instruct him? But we have the mind of Christ.

1 Corinthians 2:14-16

Overcoming Life Memory Verse

The suggested memory verse for this lesson is:

And the Word was made flesh, and dwelt among us, (and we beheld his glory, the glory as of the only begotten of the Father,) full of grace and truth.

John 1:14

Christ Unlimited — P.O. Box 850 — Dewey, AZ 86327   USA

Review Outline, Section One

I. **God's Word Is His Will**

    A. Two Greek words are translated <u>Word</u> in the Bible

       1. <u>Logos</u>

         a. God's written Word, the Bible (2 Tim. 3:16,17)

         b. Title for the Son of God (John 1:1,4; Rev. 19:13)

       2. <u>Rhema</u>

         a. Individual scriptures quickened to us by the Holy Spirit (John 6:63)

         b. Voice of the Holy Spirit in our hearts (1 John 5:6)

         c. Prophecy (1 Cor. 12:10)

            (1) Seldom for guidance; usually for confirmation

            (2) Must be tested by the written Word

       3. <u>Rhema</u> and <u>Logos</u> should always agree.

II. **God's Will Is Not Always Done**

    A. He <u>wills</u> that all be saved (2 Pet. 3:9), but all are not saved.

       1. We must <u>choose</u> whom we will serve (Josh. 24:15), and some choose the devil directly or by default.

       2. We must <u>receive</u> Jesus through faith (2 Tim. 3:15), and not all will believe.

       3. Many are called, but few are chosen (Matt. 22:14).

    B. He <u>wills</u> that all His children be healthy and well, yet not all are well (1 Thess. 5:23; 3 John 2).

       1. It was foretold that Messiah would take our sicknesses and diseases (Isa. 53:5).

Christ Unlimited — P.O. Box 850 — Dewey, AZ 86327   USA

2. Peter said Jesus did this at Calvary (1 Pet. 2:24).

3. James lists various ways provided for healing, but faith always is involved (James 5:13-16).

III. God Wants Us To Seek His Will

A. He has set two main ways of finding out His will.

1. By the written Word (2 Tim. 3:16,17)

2. By the Holy Spirit (John 16:13)

B. Wrong ways of seeking guidance

1. Opening the Bible at random, seeking a verse as direction without a total commitment to God

2. Asking God for a "sign"

   a. Circumstances

      (1) Opened doors (Rev. 3:8)

      (2) Closed doors (same reference)

   b. "Putting out a fleece" (Judg. 6:36-40)

      (1) Asking God to confirm supernaturally that a person is hearing God and not the devil, as Gideon did

      (2) A sign to find out God's will

3. Signs are the exception and are not God's norm for guidance

   a. God will sometimes honor "sign-seeking" by new or baby Christians.

   b. Seeking a sign must be done with the right attitude (Matt. 12:39,40).

Christ Unlimited — P.O. Box 850 — Dewey, AZ 86327   USA

IV. Keys to Answered Prayer

   A. Believe God will answer <u>if we ask according to His will</u> (1 John 5:14).

   B. Have a heart knowledge of the Word

      1. Memorization of scriptures is not enough (1 Cor. 2:14). (Head knowledge is not true revelation.)

      2. The Word must take root in the heart (Heb. 8:10;Luke 8:15).

      3. Delight in doing His Will in order to truly know His will (Ps. 40:8)

      4. Receive in faith, not doubting or wavering (James 1:6-8)

Christ Unlimited — P.O. Box 850 — Dewey, AZ 86327   USA

Review Outline Quiz, Section One

1. What are the two tests for any spiritual guidance?

   _____ and _____

2. What scriptures tell us this?

   _____ and _____

3. Is God's will always carried out perfectly and totally? Why not?

   _____

   _____

4. Name two things we know are His will from His Word.

   a. _____

   b. _____

5. How do we receive salvation, healing, and other things from God?

   _____

Christ Unlimited — P.O. Box 850 — Dewey, AZ 86327   USA

6. Is it a good idea to seek a "sign" from God in any way?

_____

7. What judge of Israel asked God to "prove Himself" through a supernatural sign?

_____

8. What is the main key to having our prayers answered?

_____

9. Memorizing scriptures, although good, will only give us a head _____, not a heart knowledge, of God's will.

10. What does **Psalm 40:8** tell us is another prerequisite for knowing the will of God?

_____

Christ Unlimited — P.O. Box 850 — Dewey, AZ 86327   USA

The Will of God Workbook

Section Two

"Asking According to the Word"

The Will of God Workbook
Section Two: "Asking According to the Word"
Expository Introduction

The Word of God is His will for us, and 1 John 5:14,15 tells us that if we ask anything according to His will, we may have what we ask for.

And this is the confidence that we have in him, that, if we ask any thing according to his will, he heareth us: And if we know that he hear us, whatsoever we ask, we know that we have the petitions that we desired of him.

In His Word, God has revealed what is His will and what is not His will. As an example, it is God's will for everyone to be saved and go to Heaven.

The Lord is not slack concerning his promise, as some men count slackness; but is longsuffering to us-ward, not willing that any should perish, but that all should come to repentance.

2 Peter 3:9

However, man's will for himself is not always the same as God's will for us. Therefore, not everyone is saved. God honors our choices. Too many people do not understand that choices have consequences, and the consequence, or result, of not choosing God's will to be saved is destruction and hell.

As another example, in this workbook, let us take a look at healing and at suffering.

The following scriptures tell us that it is God's will for us to be healed:

Psalm 103:3; Matt. 9:35; Mark 1:40,41; Luke 1:72, 4:18;1 Thess. 5:23; 1 Peter 2:24; and 3 John 2. (Please look up each one and examine it within its context.)

The Greek word sozo is used interchangeably for "to save" and "to heal." God does not want us to keep our sicknesses and diseases any more than He wants us to keep our sins. Isaiah 53:5 is a prophecy that Messiah would take sicknesses on Him, as well as sin, as a substitute for us.

First Peter 2:24 says that Jesus did exactly that:

Who his own self bare our sins in his own body on the tree, that we, being dead to sins, should live unto righteousness: by whose stripes ye were healed.

Therefore, we can know that legally, according to the Word of God, we can be healed as well as saved. That is not only God's will for us, but He has provided a way for us to do both.

When the Bible speaks of "taking up our crosses" or says that believers will suffer, many believers think that means God's will is for us to have the same sicknesses and diseases as the world does.

In many churches and denominations, the tradition that God brings such things on us to teach us lessons in patience, faithfulness in the midst of trials and tribulations, and steadfastness is taught as if it were Gospel. Yet that teaching cannot be found in the Bible.

Because of this erroneous teaching, however, many Christians receive sicknesses and diseases and think they are "suffering for the Lord." Anyone who truly looks at verses about the atonement will have to understand this cannot be true.

Jesus came to be both a substitute and an example for us.

In those things which He took as a substitute for us, He exchanged Himself for us, and we do not have to do those things ourselves. We do not have to die on crosses, or pay the penalty for our own sins — as long as we receive Him as our substitute. Nor do we have to endure sicknesses and diseases, as long as we receive the healing which He bought for us as a substitute.

On the other hand, His life and ministry were lived out as "examples" for us to follow:

*The Sermon on the Mount (Matt. 5,6,7) gives us the principles by which He lived.

*Mark 16:15-18 is called "the Great Commission," because in those verses, Jesus sent us to follow His example and minister as He did.

The problem comes when we mix up what He did as a substitute, which we do not have to do, and what He did as an example, which we are called to do.

There are two kinds of suffering talked about in the Bible:

*One type Christ took for us.

*The other He <u>experienced</u> as an example for us to follow. Christians need to know the difference.

Two Kinds of Suffering

The Greek word for suffer means "to bear" or "to endure." Both kinds of suffering are found in 1 Peter 4 where the Apostle Peter wrote both in the sense of bearing something and enduring something.

Beloved, think it not strange concerning the fiery trial which is to try you, as though some strange thing happened unto you: But rejoice, inasmuch as ye are partakers of Christ's sufferings; that, when his glory shall be revealed, ye may be glad also with exceeding joy. If ye be reproached for the name of Christ, happy are ye; for the spirit of glory and of God resteth upon you: on their part he is evil spoken of, but on your part he is glorified. But let none of you suffer as a murderer, or as a thief, or as an evildoer, or as a busybody in other men's matters. Yet if any man suffer as a Christian, let him not be ashamed; but let him glorify God on this behalf. Wherefore let them that suffer according to the will of God commit the keeping of their souls to him in well doing, as unto a faithful Creator.

1 Peter 4:12-16,19

Christ Unlimited — P.O. Box 850 — Dewey, AZ 86327   USA

The two kinds of suffering are:

1. Suffering because we sin, which is receiving the penalty for our own sins.

2. Suffering for Christ, which is bearing or enduring unpleasant circumstances and people for the cause of the Gospel.

When we sin, we receive the penalty of suffering for that sin because of the Law of Sowing and Reaping (Gen. 1:11,21,24; Gal. 6:7-8). However, in 1 Peter 4:15-16, the apostle wrote that believers are not to sin so that they come under the consequences. On the other hand, he said that if we suffer things — such as persecution — "as Christians" and "according to the will of God," then we should not be ashamed but glorify God.

Christ died that we might be delivered from such oppressions as sickness, fear, depression, and condemnation. However, sin in our lives can open the door for such things to attack us.

Suffering for Christ means bearing or enduring unpleasant circumstances in order to preach the Word of God. It also means enduring the company of unpleasant people in order to be witnesses of God's love. Other forms of suffering for Christ include:

1. Staying in a difficult situation for the redemption of those around you.

2. Fasting in order that something in the Kingdom of God may be accomplished.

3. Leaving our own comforts to help others in discomfort, as many missionaries have done.

4. Turning the other cheek, which means not reacting in anger or unforgiveness when someone else mistreats us and not retaliating for wrongs done us.

5. Going the second mile, continuing to help someone although the first efforts seem fruitless.

6. Getting up in the nighttime to intercede for others or to minister to those in need — thereby suffering a loss of sleep.

7. Enduring accusations without attempting to justify or defend our own actions.

8. Resisting the temptation to sin, even when the soul or the body really desires to do whatever is involved in the temptation.

As the flesh is denied, there often is suffering, but if we stand steadfast through it, we can reign victorious over those areas of temptation. Suffering for Christ is a choice we make. The Bible says if we suffer with Him, we shall reign with Him (2 Tim. 2:12).

Jesus suffered as an example for us and as a substitute for us totally by choice. When He was persecuted, He did not retaliate.

Therefore doth my Father love me, because I lay down my life, that I might take it again. No man taketh it from me, but I lay it down of myself. I have power to lay it down, and I have power to take it again. This commandment have I received of my Father.

John 10:17,18

Christ Unlimited — P.O. Box 850 — Dewey, AZ 86327   USA

For even hereunto were ye called: because Christ also suffered for us, leaving us an example, that ye should follow his steps: Who did no sin, neither was guile found in his mouth: Who, when he was reviled, reviled not again; when he suffered, he threatened not; but committed himself to him that judgeth righteously.

1 Peter 2:21-23

Likewise, in following His example, we must suffer by choice. The "martyr complex" where someone enjoys suffering, or gets self-glory out of suffering by making sure everyone around knows about it, is not what the Bible means for us to do.

Paul also suffered by choice in order for the gospel to go forth.

Then Paul answered, What mean ye to weep and to break mine heart? for I am ready not to be bound only, but also to die at Jerusalem for the name of the Lord Jesus.

Acts 21:13

If we are obedient to follow Jesus, we are going to suffer.

For unto you it is given in the behalf of Christ, not only to believe on him, but also to suffer for his sake.

Philippians 1:29

We may suffer because of unkind words, being misunderstood, or actually enduring unjust treatment. Suffering for Christ perfects us spiritually. The Bible says that Jesus Himself learned obedience through suffering (Heb. 5:8,9). The purpose of our suffering is to establish, strengthen, and settle us in the ways of God (1 Pet. 5:10). There is no other way to get the prize of the high calling of God in Christ Jesus (Phil. 3:10,14) except by suffering with Him (following His example in our lifestyles).

If God allows difficulties to remain in our lives, it is in order for us to develop a greater faith or learn to walk in the authority of Jesus by overcoming those things. God does not mean for them to be permanent (Ps. 34:19).

In order to receive healing or to walk in good health, which is our covenant right from God, we must know beyond the shadow of a doubt that <u>suffering for Christ is not suffering with sickness</u>. Because most religious people use Job as a "proof" for this wrong doctrine, let's take a look at Job's experience and see what really happened.

If we look at Job 2:7,8, we can see that the cause of the evil and sickness was Satan, not God.

> So went Satan forth from the presence of the Lord, and smote Job with sore boils from the sole of his foot to his crown. And he took him a potsherd to scrape himself withal; and he sat down among the ashes.

Also, in Job 3:25,26, we see that Job <u>did</u> have sin in his life; therefore, he had an open door for Satan to attack him. His "hedge"

Christ Unlimited — P.O. Box 850 — Dewey, AZ 86327   USA

was down. One of Job's sins was the fear he had allowed to rule him.

For the thing which I greatly feared is come upon me, and that which I was afraid of is come unto me. I was not in safety, neither had I rest, neither was I quiet; yet trouble came.

Romans 14:23 says that whatever is not of faith is of sin. Therefore, Job himself admitted that in his inner self, he had been afraid something would happen to his children. That is why he offered sacrifices so often for them (**Job 1:5**). Fear is lack of faith, and that means fear is sin.

__Fear Opens the Door to the Enemy

The Bible says that Job did not sin in what he said (**Job 1:22, 2:10**), but obviously, according to his own words, he sinned in his heart. Fear opened the door to the enemy (**Job 3:26**). Fear kept Job from walking in God's rest, in complete trust of God, so that Job was "not in safety" nor was he quiet.

Also, by reading **Job 3:1-24, 6:1-10**, and other passages, we can see that Job did not accuse God, but he did indulge in self-pity, and thought of suicide. Also, Job had a problem with self-righteousness (**Job 6:12,29,30**). In **Job 27**, he uses "I", "me", or "mine" 19 times.

Christ Unlimited — P.O. Box 850 — Dewey, AZ 86327   USA

In some of his other discussions with his "friends," we can hear the self-pity and the self-righteousness as well. Job 32:1 tells us that Job was **righteous in his own eyes**. Also, in Job 27:6, Job said he would hold fast his righteousness and his heart would not reproach him as long as he lived.

We can identify today with Job concerning three of the four friends who came to keep him company in his misery for most of us have known people like those three. They tend to accuse us, put "guilt trips" and condemnation on us, and encourage us to have the wrong attitude toward God.

Eliphas the Temanite, Bildad the Shuhite, and Zophar the Naamathite were the three men who "made an appointment" to get together and visit **Job to mourn with him and to comfort him** (Job 2:11). These three are known as "Job's Comforters." However, they certainly did not mourn "with" him nor comfort him. They were not true friends, and none of the three had an accurate explanation for Job's plight.

Job, however, did have a true friend, the fourth man who came to visit him — Elihu, son of Barachel the Buzite. Elihu's wrath was kindled, the Bible says, against Job for justifying himself rather than God. However, Elihu's wrath also was kindled against the three "friends" for condemning **Job** (Job 32:2,3).

Elihu defended God and gave Job the true answer to his ills:

Therefore hearken unto me, ye men of understanding: far be it from God, that he should do wickedness; and from the

Almighty, that he should commit iniquity. For the work of a man shall he render unto him, and cause every man to find according to his ways. ...Job hath spoken without knowledge, and his words were without wisdom. My desire is that Job may be tried unto the end because of his answers for wicked men. For he addeth rebellion unto his sin, he clappeth his hands among us, and multiplieth his words against God.

                                              Job 34:10,11,36,37

True friends will help us see our own faults in love. They will not accuse us nor condemn us. Elihu asked Job:

Thinkest thou this to be right, that thou saidst, My righteousness is more than God's?

                                              Job 35:2

In Job 37:23, Elihu pointed out to Job that God was not his problem, because God is excellent in power, and in judgment, and in plenty of justice: <u>He will not afflict</u>.

After Elihu finished, the Bible says that God Himself spoke directly to Job out of the whirlwind (Job 38:1). In Job 38-41, God asked Job some very interesting questions for which Job had no answers, such as:

*Where were you when I created the world? (v. 4)

*Who are you to talk to me without knowledge? (v. 2)

*Have you commanded night and day to exist? (12)

*Can you send lightning where it is supposed to go? (v. 35)

Christ Unlimited — P.O. Box 850 — Dewey, AZ 86327   USA

Those four chapters of Job contain some of the most revealing passages in the Bible concerning God, for He speaks there concerning what He has done and what He is like. Through God's words to Job, we get a glimpse of how God thinks. Through His conversation in those chapters, God convicted Job of pride and contrasted human abilities and knowledge with His own.

In the end, of course, Job recognized his sins (fear, self-pity, self-righteousness, rebellion against chastisement, and pride) and repented (**Job 42:1-6**). Upon Job's true repentance, God not only put a stop to Satan's attacks but restored to Job a double portion of herds and the same number of sons and daughters as he had before (**Job 42:12,13**).

Through looking at Job, we can see that God did not afflict Job nor was what happened His perfect will for Job. However, Job's sins caused God to allow the devil, because of an open door, to attack Job in all areas except taking his life (**Job 2:6**).

We, as Christians, do not need to suffer as Job did, if we simply cry out for a heart cleansing and stay away from sin, particularly the sin of pride that David called "the great transgression" (**Ps. 19:13**).

From this look at Job, and from the fact that we can see healing was provided in the atonement (**Isa. 53:5; 1 Pet. 2:24**), it should be very plain that it is never God's will for us to be sick.

However, another "proof" people use who believe God's will is for us to experience sickness and disease is the Apostle Paul's reference to his "thorn in the flesh." So let's take a look at what Paul actually said that is so misinterpreted and, from the context, let's see what he meant.

Christ Unlimited — P.O. Box 850 — Dewey, AZ 86327   USA

What Is a "Thorn in the Flesh?"

In **2 Corinthians 12:7-10**, Paul referred to a "thorn in the flesh" by which he was "buffeted" in order that he would not get into pride (v.7) because of his abundant revelations from Jesus.

The thing we must understand is that "Paul's thorn in the flesh," contrary to common belief, was not sickness but an <u>individual</u>. We can see that is true for two reasons:

1. Common usage of that phrase
2. The Bible's interpretation of the phrase

A thorn in the flesh, or a "thorn in the side," is a figure of speech that is still used today. Even after almost two thousand years, that phrase is not used to refer to sicknesses, financial problems, or other intangible situations. It always is used when referring to a <u>person</u>.

We hear people today say, "That person who works with me (or is a family member, or an in-law, or a neighbor, or someone in the local church) is a real thorn in my side." In **Joshua 23:13**, harrassing nations were referred to as "snares, traps, scourges, and thorns." In **Ezekiel 28:24**, Judah's enemies were described as thorns.

And there shall be no more a <u>pricking briar</u> unto the house of Israel, nor any grieving thorn of all that are round about them, that depised them; and they shall know that I am the Lord God.

Christ Unlimited — P.O. Box 850 — Dewey, AZ 86327   USA

In **2 Cor. 12:7** Paul explained what his "thorn in the flesh" was:

...There was given (assigned) to me a thorn in the flesh, <u>the messenger of Satan to buffet me</u>, lest I should be exalted above measure.

<u>A messenger of Satan</u> was a demonic spirit that followed Paul on his travels influencing a person or persons to speak against him and, if possible, to arouse persecution against him. From these verses, we can see that the <u>thorn</u> was someone with an evil spirit who was speaking against Paul. A "messenger" is someone who speaks a message, so Paul was receiving a buffeting or "tongue-lashing" from someone contending against him.

To <u>buffet</u> means "to strike, beat, or keep under." Therefore, a <u>buffeting</u> would be something coming against Paul from the outside, as the wind buffets a ship. This is not referring to a sickness on the inside. And, apparently, even Paul was aware that he had a tendency toward pride that allowed this attack. Eventually, however, we see that Paul was able to mature and overcome his persecutions and afflictions, of whatever sort (**2 Tim. 3:11**).

People say, "Yes, but Paul talked about his <u>infirmities</u>, and infirmities are sicknesses and diseases."

That is true in <u>our</u> time. Today, we almost exclusively use <u>infirmities</u> as a synonym for "sickness." However, it was not true of the original Greek. <u>Vine's Dictionary</u> gives us two words for <u>infirmity</u>: <u>astheneia</u>, singular, and <u>asthenema</u>, plural.[1]

Christ Unlimited — P.O. Box 850 — Dewey, AZ 86327   USA

The singular word literally means "want of strength, weakness, indicating inability to produce results." Obviously that can mean other things than physical disabilities. The plural word means "those scruples which arise through weakness of faith."

Vine added, "The strong must support the infirmities of the weak by submitting to self-restraint" (Rom. 15:1).

Strong's New Exhaustive Concordance says that these words are used for sicknesses or disease by implication.[2] In other words, we need to look at the context in which the word is used to find whether sicknesses or weaknesses of other kinds, such as lack of faith, is meant.

Paul wrote that he had sought God three times to have "it" (the messenger of Satan) removed, and God's answer was always,"...**My grace is sufficient for thee: for my strength is made perfect in weakness...**" (2 Cor. 12:9). Therefore, Paul decided that he would "gladly" glory and take pleasure in his <u>infirmities</u>, reproaches, needs, persecutions, and distresses <u>for Christ's sake</u> (2 Cor. 12:10). That meant he was suffering for Jesus in the sense that he was following Jesus' example in the way he ministered and lived out his life. Because of that, he had persecutions and distresses.

The context plainly shows that Paul was not referring to some sickness that he could not get over and of which God refused to heal him. Paul was saying:

"When I am weak, the Lord makes me strong. When I cannot do something, He enables me to do it. When I cannot overcome, He overcomes through me, and when I cannot deal with, escape from, or remove the person who is persecuting me, God will give me the grace to bear it."

There <u>was</u> a time when Paul did have a temporary "infirmity of the flesh," or a sickness, but it was not permanent, nor was it his "thorn in the flesh." **Galatians 4:13,14** says:

> Ye know how through infirmity of the flesh I preached the gospel unto you at the first. And my temptation which was in my flesh ye despised not nor rejected; but received me as an angel of God, even as Christ Jesus.

Paul even calls this "infirmity of the flesh" a <u>temptation</u>, or trial, showing that sickness is something to be resisted and overcome.

God's Way of Chastising His Children

Those who believe or teach that sickness is God's will say that it is His way of chastening us. However, we have seen from the book of Job that God did not chastise Job with disaster, destruction of his herds and children, loss of wealth, or loss of his health. The Bible says very plainly that Satan did that. We have seen that Job did have sins of attitudes that created "holes" in his security in God (Psalm 91). The same thing was true of Paul.

However, God <u>did</u> chastise Job, and we need to look at that and see how God chastises His children. God chastised Job with His words (Job 38-41). He spoke to Job and directed Job's attention to Himself.

Christ Unlimited — P.O. Box 850 — Dewey, AZ 86327   USA

Chastisement is not punishment but instruction.

God instructed Job, and Job received God's rhema (spoken) word as revelation. God's chastising illuminated Job to himself as well as showed him things about God that he had not understood.

The Greek word translated chastise in Hebrews 12:4-11 — the verses that plainly spell out why God chastens us — primarily means "to train children." It suggests educating by correcting with words, by "reproving, admonishing, and instructing."

God chastises us today by His written Word and through the Holy Spirit. If, knowing His ways and His Word we still are disobedient and rebellious, the enemy can gain access to us, just as he did to Job.

In those verses in Hebrews, the writer quoted Proverbs 3:11,12, which say that God chastens (instructs, reproves, or admonishes) those whom He loves. If a believer is not being chastised by God, then he is not a true believer but "illegitimate" (Heb. 12:8).

God perfects — or sanctifies — us through several means:

*He sanctifies or cleanses us by His Word.

Sanctify them through thy truth: thy word is truth.

John 17:17

*He purges and cleanses us by the Word, which is sharp enough to divide spirit and soul (Heb. 4:12) and discern the "thoughts and intents" of the heart.

Christ Unlimited — P.O. Box 850 — Dewey, AZ 86327   USA

Every branch in me that beareth not fruit he taketh away: and every branch that beareth fruit, he purgeth it, that it may bring forth more fruit. Now ye are clean through the word which I have spoken unto you.

John 15:2,3

Wherewithal shall a young man cleanse his way? by taking heed thereto according to thy word.

Psalm 119:9

Husbands, love your wives, even as Christ also loved the church, and gave himself for it; That he might sanctify and cleanse it with the washing of water by the word.

Ephesians 5:25,26

*God purifies us through our obedience to the truth.

Seeing ye have purified your souls in obeying the truth through the Spirit unto unfeigned love of the brethren, see that ye love one another with a pure heart fervently.

1 Peter 1:22

*God sanctifies us by our faith in Him.

Christ Unlimited — P.O. Box 850 — Dewey, AZ 86327   USA

And God, which knoweth the hearts, bare them witness, giving them the Holy Ghost, even as he did unto us: And put no difference between us and them, purifying their hearts by faith.

To open their eyes, and to turn them from darkness to light, and from the power of Satan unto God, that they may receive forgiveness of sins, and inheritance among them which are sanctified by faith that is in me.

Acts 15:8,9; 26:18

*God perfects, edifies, and teaches His children through the five-fold ministry gifts to the Body of Christ.

And he gave some, apostles; and some, prophets; and some, evangelists; and some, pastors and teachers; For the perfecting of the saints, for the work of the ministry, for the edifying of the body of Christ: Till we all come in the unity of the faith, and of the knowledge of the Son of God, unto a perfect man, unto the measure of the stature of the fulness of Christ: That we henceforth be no more children, tossed to and fro, and carried about with every wind of doctrine, by the sleight of men, and cunning craftiness, whereby they lie in wait to deceive. But, speaking the truth in love, may grow up into him in all things, which is the head, even Christ.

Ephesians 4:11-15

Christ Unlimited — P.O. Box 850 — Dewey, AZ 86327   USA

*God teaches us through His scriptures.

All scripture is given by inspiration of God, and is profitable for doctrine, for reproof, for correction, for instruction in righteousness: That the man of God may be perfect, thoroughly furnished unto all good works.

2 Timothy 3:16,17

This is what Paul meant when he wrote for believers to "work out" their salvation. He was not talking about salvation of the spirit, which is a free gift from God. He was talking about our souls, or personalities, being perfected in the image of Jesus.

Wherefore, my beloved, as ye have always obeyed, not as in my presence only, but now much more in my absence, work out your own salvation with fear and trembling. For it is God which worketh in you both to will and to do of his good pleasure. Do all things without murmurings and disputings: That ye may be blameless and harmless, the sons of God, without rebuke, in the midst of a crooked and perverse nation, among whom ye shine as lights in the world. Holding forth the word of life; that I may rejoice in the day of Christ, that I have not run in vain, neither laboured in vain.

Philippians 2:12-16

Consequences of Disobedience

What are the consequences of a believer's not learning God's ways and failing to obey God's Word?

The consequences of <u>ignorance</u>, or lack of knowledge about God's ways is destruction.

My people are destroyed for lack of knowledge...

Hosea 4:6

Second Timothy 2:15 says that we should study the Word in order not to be ashamed. Therefore, ignorance can bring humiliation.

The consequences of knowing what is right and not doing it willingly is destruction also.

If ye be willing and obedient, ye shall eat of the good of the land: But if ye refuse and rebel, ye shall be devoured with the sword: for the mouth of the Lord hath spoken it.

Isaiah 1:19,20

If we obey God, we will <u>not</u> reap evil.

Therefore now amend your ways and your doings, and obey the voice of the Lord your God; and the Lord will repent him of the evil that he hath pronounced against you.

Jeremiah 26:13

We should not be robbed of joy, peace, finances, health, and other blessings. Deuteronomy 30:19,20 says that if we choose life (obedience), we will be blessed; but, if we choose disobedience, we will receive the curse of the law.

I call heaven and earth to record this day against you, that I have set before you life and death, blessing and cursing: therefore choose life, that both thou and thy seed may live: That thou mayest love the Lord thy God, and that thou mayest obey his voice, and that thou mayest cleave unto him: for he is thy life, and the length of thy days: that thou mayest dwell in the land which the Lord sware unto thy fathers, to Abraham, to Isaac, and to Jacob to give them.

Therefore, we see that not only is it not God's will for us to live in ignorance or disobedience but that it is not His fault if consequences come upon us. What we sow, we will reap.

Be not deceived; God is not mocked: for whatsoever a man soweth, that shall he also reap.

Galatians 6:7

It is the goodness of God that leads a man to repentance; but, it is the hardness of men's hearts that stirs the wrath of God and brings His judgment down on individuals and nations.

Christ Unlimited — P.O. Box 850 — Dewey, AZ 86327   USA

But we are sure that the judgment of God is according to truth against them which commit such things. And thinkest thou this, O man, that judgest them which do such things, and doest the same, that thou shalt escape the judgment of God? Or despisest thou the riches of his goodness and forbearance and longsuffering; not knowing that the goodness of God leadeth thee to repentance? But after thy hardness and impenitent heart treasurest up unto thyself wrath against the day of wrath and revelation of the righteous judgment of God; Who will render to every man according to his deeds:

Romans 2:2-6

If we are to be blessed and not cursed, we must be doers of the Word and not hearers only.

But be ye doers of the word, and not hearers only, deceiving your own selves. For if any be a hearer of the word, and not a doer, he is like unto a man beholding his natural face in a glass: For he beholdeth himself, and goeth his way, and straightway forgetteth what manner of man he was.

James 1:22-24

God's wrath is the "curse of the law" which is the penalty for sin.

Behold therefore the goodness and severity of God: on them which fell, severity; but toward thee, goodness, if thou continue

Christ Unlimited — P.O. Box 850 — Dewey, AZ 86327   USA

in his goodness: otherwise thou also shalt be cut off.

Romans 11:22

If we persist in disobedience, then our own wickedness will correct us (Jer. 2:19).

God's Word does not specifically answer such questions as, "Is this person the right mate for me?" or "Should I go into full-time ministry?" The Bible does show us a pattern for receiving God's guidance in personal matters in Romans 12:1-3.

The first step in this pattern is to present ourselves as <u>living sacrifices</u> to God, which means a "total commitment." That involves "bearing our crosses daily" (Luke 9:23-27, 14:26-33). As we have seen, bearing our crosses does not mean sickness, poverty, or sin. It is not an unsaved spouse nor a bothersome individual. The "cross" we are to bear every day is giving up our will for His. We are to die daily to self-will and live for Christ's will.

I beseech you therefore, brethren, by the mercies of God, that ye present your bodies a living sacrifice, holy, acceptable unto God, which is your reasonable service. And be not conformed to this world: but be ye transformed by the renewing of your mind, that ye may prove what is that good, and acceptable, and perfect, will of God. For I say, through the grace given unto me, to every man that is among you, not to think of himself more highly than he ought to think; but to think soberly, according as God hath dealt to every man the measure of faith.

The second step toward finding God's will is the renewing of our minds.

And be renewed in the spirit of your mind.

Ephesians 4:23

To do this, we <u>must</u> spend time in the Bible in order for our thoughts to begin to line up with God's thoughts and not with the world's thinking. At some point, if we really study the Word asking for inspiration and understanding from the Holy Spirit, there will come a time when we really <u>delight</u> in doing God's will (**Ps. 40:8**). We can have the mind of Christ.

But the natural man receiveth not the things of the Spirit of God: for they are foolishness unto him: neither can he know them, because they are spiritually discerned. But he that is spiritual judgeth all things, yet he himself is judged of no man. For who hath known the mind of the Lord, that he may instruct him? But we have the mind of Christ.

1 Corinthians 2:14-16

The third step in finding God's will is to be willing to prove or test our decisions in the light of His Word. If any decision contradicts God's Word, we can know immediately that the decision is wrong. God always answers according to the principles of the Scripture. God will lead us by His Word and by the Holy Spirit, not primarily by "signs" or circumstances.

Christ Unlimited — P.O. Box 850 — Dewey, AZ 86327   USA

We must approach God with humility when we seek His guidance. Spiritual pride, which is trusting in one's own knowledge instead of God, is the downfall of many men. Also, spiritual pride could be defined as "faith in our faith." In other words, we trust primarily in ourselves, making "faith" a matter of striving or works.

We must seek God's will with sober minds, or spiritually reasonable minds. God is a logical, reasonable God, not the author of confusion (1 Cor. 14:33). A prequisite for getting answers from God is to truly commit the matters on which we are seeking guidance to Him and be truly willing to obey His will. The final ingredient in finding God's will is faith. We must believe that God will reveal His will to us. In other words, we must seek Him wholeheartedly (Jer. 29:11-13).

Knowing God's will is not an automatic thing. It requires trust, obedience, study of His Word, prayer, total commitment, and earnestly seeking Him. There are no easy formulas, only a daily walk with Him will allow us to know His will for our lives.

Christ Unlimited — P.O. Box 850 — Dewey, AZ 86327   USA

Endnotes

[1]Vine, W. E. <u>Vine's Expository Dictionary of Old and New Testament Words</u> (Old Tappan: Fleming H. Revell, 1981), Vol. 2, p. 257.

[2]Strong, James. <u>The New Strong's Exhaustive Concordance of the Bible</u>, "Greek Dictionary of the New Testament" (Nashville: Thomas Nelson Publishers, 1984), p. 16.

Christ Unlimited — P.O. Box 850 — Dewey, AZ 86327   USA

Lesson for Section Two

[Author's Note: All Scripture references that answer these questions have been given. Please do not look at the answer page until you have answered the questions in your own words. This is not a test, but an expository lesson to help you learn.]

I. God's Will for Us in Matters of Health

A. God's will is for all to be saved and _____.

Reference: 2 Peter 3:9

1. What two meanings does the Greek word sozo have in the New Testament? (See Expository Introduction.)

_____ and _____

2. Why are some not healed and not saved?

_____

B. What does God's Word say about His will for us concerning healing?

_____

Beloved, I wish above all things that thou mayest prosper and be in health, even as thy soul prospereth.

3 John 1:2

Christ Unlimited — P.O. Box 850 — Dewey, AZ 86327   USA

And the very God of peace sanctify you wholly; and I pray God your whole spirit, soul, and body be preserved blameless unto the coming of our Lord Jesus Christ.

1 Thessalonians 5:23

Who his own self bare our sins in his own body on the tree, that we, being dead to sins, should live unto righteousness: by whose stripes ye were healed.

1 Peter 2:24

Who forgiveth all thine iniquities; who healeth all thy diseases.

Psalm 103:3

The Spirit of the Lord is upon me, because he hath anointed me to preach the gospel to the poor; he hath sent me to heal the brokenhearted, to preach deliverance to the captives, and recovering of sight to the blind, to set at liberty them that are bruised.

Luke 4:18

And Jesus went about all the cities and villages, teaching in their synagogues, and preaching the gospel of the kingdom, and healing every sickness and every disease among the people.

Matthew 9:35

Christ Unlimited — P.O. Box 850 — Dewey, AZ 86327   USA

1. What Old Testament verse prophesied that Jesus would take our sicknesses as well as our sins?_____

2. What New Testament verse tells us this was accomplished?

_____

II. God's Will for Us Concerning Suffering

   A. There are two kinds of suffering mentioned in the Bible. What are they?

      1. _____

      2. _____

         a. What does the Greek word translated "suffering" mean?
            "To _____ or "to _____

         b. Which suffering did Jesus come to deliver us from?

            _____

But let none of you suffer as a murderer, or as a thief, or as an evildoer, or as a busybody in other men's matters.

1 Peter 4:15

         c. What did Christ give us so that we do not have to suffer under Satan's hand?

            _____

Christ Unlimited — P.O. Box 850 — Dewey, AZ 86327   USA

Behold, I give unto you power to tread on serpants and scorpions, and over all the power of the enemy; and nothing shall by any means hurt you.

Luke 10:19

Submit yourselves therefore to God. Resist the devil, and he will flee from you.

James 4:7

And Jesus answered and said unto him, Get thee behind me, Satan: for it is written, Thou shalt worship the Lord thy God, and him only shalt thou serve.

Luke 4:8

B. When do we suffer _for_ Christ?

_____

1. Suffering for Christ is the same thing as:

_____

And he said to them all, If any man will come after me, let him deny himself, and take up his cross daily, and follow me. . . . And whosoever doth not bear his cross, and come after me, cannot be my disciple.

Luke 9:23; 14:27

2. Name some of the ways that we might suffer for Christ:

_____

_____

_____

_____

_____

_____

3. Does God make us suffer for Jesus, or is it by our own choices?

_____

References: Philippians 1:29, 1 Peter 2:21-24

a. Did Jesus suffer by choice? _____

Therefore doth my Father love me, because I lay down my life, that I might take it again. No man taketh it from me, but I lay it down of myself. I have power to lay it down, and I have power to take it again. This commandment have I received of my Father.

John 10:17,18

Christ Unlimited — P.O. Box 850 — Dewey, AZ 86327   USA

b. Did Paul suffer by his own choice? _____

Then Paul answered, What mean ye to weep and to break mine heart? for I am ready not to be bound only, but also to die at Jerusalem for the name of the Lord Jesus.

Acts 21:13

C. Bearing our crosses daily and following Jesus' example of suffering allows God to _____ us.

1. How did Jesus "learn" obedience? _____

2. Through suffering, Jesus became the _____ of eternal salvation to those who _____ Him. Reference:

Though he were a Son, yet learned he obedience by the things which he suffered; And being made perfect, he became the author of eternal salvation unto all them that obey him.

Hebrews 5:8,9

III. Exposing the Lie That Sickness Is God's Will

A. What Old Testament hero is wrongly used as "proof" for the false doctrine that God "teaches" us through sickness?

_____

1. Who actually was the author of Job's suffering?

   _____

   Reference: **Job 2:6,7**

2. Why was Satan allowed to attack Job?

   _____

3. Job did not sin with his lips, at least in the beginning of his trials, but what was in his heart? _____
   Reference: **Job 3:25**

4. In addition to <u>fear</u>, what other sinful attitudes of the heart showed up in Job as the situation progressed?

   _____

   _____

   References: **Job 6:9,7:11,13:15,27:6,30:20-21,32:2,34: 35,35:2,12,13,16**

5. Did Job's first three friends speak truth and comfort him (Job 32:3)? _____ Name the three friends.
   a. _____
   b. _____
   c. _____
      Reference: **Job 2:11**

Christ Unlimited — P.O. Box 850 — Dewey, AZ 86327   USA

6. Name Job's true friend, who dared to speak truth to him and defend God: _____

Reference: Job 32:1,2

   a. Elihu said God will not _____ us.

   b. He also said God has _____ of justice.
     Reference: Job 37:23

7. Who else spoke to Job of his sinful attitudes and really straightened him out in his thinking? _____

Reference: Job 38-41

   a. What main sin did God deal with Job personally about?

   _____

   b. In those chapters, God made it plain who was the _____ and who was the creature.

8. How did Job get out of his troubles?

_____

Reference: Job 42:1-6

Christ Unlimited — P.O. Box 850 — Dewey, AZ 86327   USA

9. What was the end result after Satan's attack on Job?

_____

Reference: Job 42:10-17

B. Who is the New Testament apostle wrongly used by some Christians as "proof" that God puts sickness on us?

_____

1. Scripturally, what was Paul's "thorn in the flesh"

_____

Reference: 2 Corinthians 12:7-10

a. Why did the Lord not remove this person from Paul's life?

_____

Reference: 2 Corinthians 12:7

b. Did Paul eventually overcome his afflictions and persecutions? _____
Reference: 2 Timothy 3:11

2. Who did God call "thorns, briers, scourges, and traps" through Joshua and Ezekiel?

_____

References: Joshua 23:13; Ezekiel 28:24

Christ Unlimited — P.O. Box 850 — Dewey, AZ 86327   USA

3. What did Paul mean by "glorying in his infirmities"?

_____

_____

   a. What does the Greek word translated infirmities mean?

     _____

   b. The modern usage of <u>infirmities</u> which is _____ has confused this issue.

IV. God's Way of Chastisement

   A. How does God chastise His children?

     _____

     Reference: **Hebrews 12:4-11**

     1. Does God mean us to be defeated in life? _____
       Reference: **Psalm 34:19; Rom. 5:17**

     2. What does the Greek word translated "chastise" mean? (See expository introduction.)

     _____

B. How does God cleanse, perfect, teach, or admonish us?

_____

References: John 15:2,3, 17:17; Psalm 119:9; 1 Peter 1:22; Acts 15: 8,9, 26:18; Ephesians 4:11-15, 5:25,26; 2 Timothy 3:16,17

V. Consequences of Obedience and Disobedience

A. We must learn as Jesus, our example, did.

1. Jesus learned by _____

Reference: Hebrews 5:8,9

2. We are to _____ the Lord for things to go well with us.

Reference: Jeremiah 38:20

B. What are two other ways we can learn about God?

1. _____

References: 2 Timothy 2:15; Psalm 119

2. _____

Reference: Matthew 19:17b

C. What happens if we do not learn or do not obey?

1. _____

   Reference: Hosea 4:6

2. _____

   Reference: 2 Timothy 2:15

3. _____

   Reference: Isaiah 1:19,20

4. _____

   Reference: Jeremiah 26:13; Romans 2:2-6, 11:22

   a. According to James 1:22-25, we are to be _____
      _____ of the Word.

   b. Then we will be _____.

D. If we persist in our disobedience, then our own _____
   _____ will correct us.
   References: Jeremiah 2:19, 5:3-6

E. What is the penalty of sin as a result of sowing and
   reaping, according to Romans 2:2-6, 11:22 and Gal. 6:7-8?

_____

Christ Unlimited — P.O. Box 850 — Dewey, AZ 86327   USA

Overcoming Life Memory Verse

The suggested memory verse for this section is :

Many are the afflictions of the righteous: but the Lord delivereth him out of them all.

Psalm 34:19

Christ Unlimited — P.O. Box 850 — Dewey, AZ 86327   USA

Review Outline, Section Two

I. The Truth About God's Will for Us

    A. God's will is for all mankind to be saved (2 Pet. 3:9;

       1 Tim. 2:4).

      1. All men are not saved.

      2. Many exercise their rights to choose against God.

    B. God's will is for all of His children to be healed

       (Ps. 103:3; 1 Thess. 5:23; 3 John 1,2).

    C. We are saved and/or healed by our choices to receive what already has been provided for us at Calvary.

      1. We receive anything from God <u>by faith</u>.

        a. We must believe God <u>exists</u> and that He loves us (John 3:16).

        b. We must believe that we have a right to blessings under the blood covenant through Jesus (Gal. 3:29).

        c. We must ask in faith for what we need and desire (Matt. 7:7 Mark 11:23-24).

      2. We must know how to apply the scriptures, which tell us what God has for us (2 Tim. 2:15).

      3. We must "follow God's rules" of hearing and obeying Him (Deut. 29:9; Acts 5:29).

II. The Truth About Suffering

    A. True suffering for Christ is always a choice.

      1. Jesus is our example (John 10:17,18).

      2. Paul chose to go to Jerusalem even after a prophecy that he would be arrested (Acts 21:13).

Christ Unlimited — P.O. Box 850 — Dewey, AZ 86327   USA

    3. We suffer by <u>choosing</u> God's will over our own, just as Jesus did in the Garden of Gethsemane (**Luke 22:42**).

  B. Having sicknesses or diseases is not "suffering for Jesus."

    1. Jesus bore the penalty for sin on the cross, so we are no longer under the curse (**Heb. 9:12**).

    2. Jesus also bore our infirmities (weaknesses in all areas, including health) on the cross (**Isa. 53:5; 1 Pet. 2:24**).

  C. Different kinds of suffering in the Bible (**1 Pet. 4:15,16**)

    1. Suffering as the result of broken spiritual or physical laws

      a. Sickness, depression, fear, poverty, broken relationships, and so forth.

      b. Reaping what has been sown by our own and other's sins (**Gal. 6:7**).

      c. Being yoked unequally with unbelievers (**2 Cor. 6:14**).

    2. Sacrificing for the sake of the gospel

      a. Leaving family and friends, comfortable surroundings, and financial security to preach the Word of God.

      b. Persecution for the Word's sake (**Matt, 13:21**).

    3. Suffering because the flesh resists temptation (**Heb. 11:24-25**).

  D. Discern between Satan's attacks and enduring suffering for Christ's sake (**James 4:7,8**).

    1. Approach God with a submissive attitude.

    2. Avoid doublemindedness.

    3. God always gives us grace to endure.

    4. Lack of knowledge of the Bible can open the door to Satan.

Christ Unlimited — P.O. Box 850 — Dewey, AZ 86327   USA

E. We should follow Jesus' example (Heb. 5:8,9) and:

    1. Bear or endure things for His sake.

    2.Not suffer things which He took as our substitute (Heb. 2:9,14,17, 10:10,14). Those are things like:

        a. Our sins (Isa. 53:1-8).

        b. Sicknesses and diseases (1 Pet. 2:24).

F. Jesus never suffered with sicknesses or disease.

    1.He resisted temptation through fasting, prayer, and speaking the Word of God to the tempter (Matt. 4:1-10).

    2. He endured the highest kind of suffering (Heb. 12:2).

        a. We should following His example with a complete commitment (John 15:19-21; Phil. 1:29).

        b. We should totally die to self as He did (Luke 9:23-27).

G. Suffering is a prerequisite to reigning with Jesus (2 Tim. 2:11,12).

    1. Suffering is part of the high calling (Phil. 3:10-14).

    2. Overcomers gain grace and joy in suffering (Heb. 12:2).

III. The Truth About the Suffering of Job and Paul

A. Job was afflicted by Satan, not God (Job 2:7).

    1. Job's hedge had "holes" in it:
fear, self-pity, self-righteousness, pride (Job 32:1; 35:2).

    2. In spite of this, God was proud of Job (Job 1:8, 2:3).

        a. He was blessed (Job 1:1-3).

        b. He did not sin with his words at first (Job 2:10); later, the workings of his heart came out (Job 3:25, 32:1, 34:5, 35:2).

c. Conclusion: The closer one walks to God, the more Satan hunts for hidden sins as "open doors" to attack.

3. Job had four friends, who came to keep him company (Job 2:11, 32:1,2).

   a. The first three friends did not give good advice (Job 32:3).

   b. The fourth friend rebuked Job and defended God (Job 34:35-37, 37:23).

4. God Himself admonished Job (Job 38-41).

   a. Job repented (Job 42:1-6).

   b. He interceded for the three friends (Job 42:8-10).

   c. Job was restored a double portion of goods and the same number of children again (Job 42:10-17).

B. Paul was afflicted by a messenger of Satan (2 Cor. 12:7-10).

1. A "thorn in the flesh" refers to a person, or people.

   a. Nations against Israel and Judah were called thorns also. (Josh. 23:13; Ezk. 28:24).

   b. Today, the phrase is used about people too.

2. Paul was afflicted because of an "open door" of pride (2 Cor.12:7).

   a. There was a time when Paul had a temporary "infirmity of the flesh," but it was not permanent nor "a thorn in the flesh" (Gal. 4:13,14).

      (1) Paul even called that "infirmity of the flesh" a <u>temptation</u> (trial) (Gal. 4:14).

      (2) When he went to God, Paul was given a "remedy."

Christ Unlimited — P.O. Box 850 — Dewey, AZ 86327   USA

3. The remedy was to trust God's strength in areas where he was weak (2 Cor. 12:10).

   a. Our weaknesses (infirmities) make room for God's grace.

   b. The meaning of <u>infirmities</u> is weaknesses in any area of life.

V. God's Way of Chastising His Children (Heb. 12:4-11)

   A. The Greek word translated <u>chastise</u> means "to instruct."

      1. God chastises us by His Word and His Spirit.

      2. He never punishes us with sicknesses.

   B. There are two pathways of learning in life (Matt. 7:13-14).

      1. The easy way: hearing and willingly obeying God's Word from the heart, not works (Isa. 1:19).

      2. The hard way: trial and error (Prov. 14:12).

   C. God perfects, cleanses, sanctifies, and purifies us by:

      1. His Word (2 Tim. 2:15; Ps. 119).

      2. Following Jesus' example (Heb. 5:8,9).

         a. Conforming to His image (Rom. 8:29, 12:2).

         b. Laying aside our old natures (Col. 3:9).

         c. Suffering persecution and tribulations here for His sake (Acts 14:22; Rom. 5:3).

      3. Hearing and obeying God (James 1:22-25)

   D. Disobedience brings consequences, such as:

      1. Destruction (Hos. 4:6).

      2. Shame (2 Tim. 2:15).

      3. The penalty of sin, which is the wrath of God (Rom. 2:2-6, 11:22).

Christ Unlimited — P.O. Box 850 — Dewey, AZ 86327   USA

E. If we are faithful, God promises to deliver us out of all afflictions (Ps. 34:19).

Christ Unlimited — P.O. Box 850 — Dewey, AZ 86327   USA

Review Outline Quiz, Section Two

1. What is the kind of suffering Christians are called to do?

   _____

2. What is the part we must do to be saved and healed?

   _____

3. What is the highest kind of suffering?

   _____

4. Why must we suffer in order to reign with Jesus?

   _____

5. Who afflicted Job and Paul?

   _____

6. Was Paul's "thorn in the flesh" a sickness or disease?_____
   What was it?

   _____

   _____

7. How could Satan attack these two great men of God?

   _____

   _____

8. How does God chastise us?

   _____

9. What are some consequences of disobedience?

   _____

10. What scripture says God promises to deliver us out of all
    afflictions?

    _____

What You Need to Know About
Christ Unlimited Ministries

Purpose and Vision

Go ye therefore, and teach all nations, baptizing them in the name of the Father, and of the Son, and of the Holy Ghost: Teaching them to observe all things whatsoever I have commanded you: and, lo, I am with you always, even unto the end of the world. Amen.

Matthew 28:19, 20

CHRIST UNLIMITED is not "another denomination," sect, or just a separate group. It is an arm of the Body of Christ — the Church of Jesus Christ, which has been called to strengthen the Body at large. We also believe we have been called to help establish the Kingdom of God in the earth.

CHRIST UNLIMITED is open to help and work with all Bible-believing Christians regardless of their church or denominational affiliations and committed to helping wherever possible in evangelistic and teaching outreaches.

CHRIST UNLIMITED believes that time is running out and the Gospel has not been preached to every creature. Many nations have not heard the Gospel, and in many places, doors for evangelism are closing. We believe it is time all Christians cooperated with the Lord in breaking down denominational walls for a united front line against the kingdom of darkness and in setting up the Kingdom of the Lord Jesus Christ by the power of the Holy Spirit.

CHRIST UNLIMITED provides such tools as to enable the saints of God to establish the Kingdom of God in the earth. We encourage groups of prayer warriors who will pray, fast, and intercede for the nations. This, we believe, is weapon number one. We teach believers how to overcome through spiritual warfare and through knowing how to use their authority in Christ Jesus through the Word and the power of the Holy Spirit.

Christians need to know how to bring down the forces of darkness in their own lives and in the lives of those to whom they minister. We provide such tools as Bibles, literature, CHRIST UNLIMITED books, and downloadable audio and video. We promote the Gospel going forth via any means of communication, including radio and video, the INTERNET, and literature. We promote teaching seminars, Bible schools, and correspondence courses, all aimed at winning souls to Christ and building the Body of Christ into maturity.

Bud and Betty Miller serve the Lord together as founders of the multi-vision ministry outreach, CHRIST UNLIMITED. The outreaches of this ministry have stemmed from a tremendous desire to see the Word of God taught in its balanced entirety. The Millers are firm believers in prayer and, through prayer, have seen many released from the bondages of fear, failure, and defeat.

Christ Unlimited — P.O. Box 850 — Dewey, AZ 86327 USA

The Millers have a world-wide vision for spreading the full-gospel message and teaching God's Word. Bud not only preaches and pastors a church, but is director of **CHRIST UNLIMITED PUBLISHING**, an outreach dedicated to publishing God's Word in many languages. His experience, openness to the Holy Spirit, and down-to-earth expression of God's love have blessed many. God has endowed Betty with a rare gift of teaching that makes her a practical and effective "handmaiden of the Lord." Both Bud and Betty have hearts turned toward evangelism and missions, desiring to tell everyone of God's wonderful love. Their anointed teaching comes across with simplicity and in the power of the Holy Spirit.

The outreaches of **CHRIST UNLIMITED** are in obedience to the words of our Lord in **Mark 16:15: Go ye into all the world and preach the gospel to every creature.** This mandate from the Lord presents a challenge to our generation as an estimated 25 percent of the world's population still have not heard the Good News of Jesus Christ.[1]

CHRIST UNLIMITED MINISTRIES also is dedicated to teaching God's Word. **Hosea 4:6** says: **My people are destroyed for lack of knowledge.** Many Christians are leading defeated lives simply because they do not know God's Word in its fullest.

CHRIST UNLIMITED MINISTRIES has provided literature for those who desire to know God's Word in a greater way. The main thrust of the teaching and literature is directed at "How to be an overcomer." In the endtimes, we must be prepared to overcome the onslaughts of Satan. Many Christians are suffering needlessly, because they do not know how to overcome sin, sickness, depression, divorce, fear, and financial failure. **CHRIST UNLIMITED MINISTRIES** provides answers for troubled families as well as trains workers for service.

DOCTRINAL STATEMENT

> Jesus answered them, and said, My doctrine is not mine, but his that sent me. If any man will do his will, he shall know of the doctrine, whether it be of God, or whether I speak of myself.
>
> John 7:16,17

Inspiration of Scriptures: We believe that the Holy Bible is the written Word of the Living God. We believe it was inspired by the Holy Spirit and recorded by holy men of old. It is infallible in content and a perfect treasure of heavenly instruction which is truth without any mixture of error. The Bible reveals the principles by which God will judge us and reveals His great plan of salvation. It will remain eternally. We believe the Bible is the true center of Christian union and the supreme standard by which all human conduct, creeds, and opinions should be tried. Therefore, we believe this Word should go into all the world and should be given first place in every believer's life (**2 Tim. 3:16; Heb. 4:12; 1 Pet. 1:23-25; and 2 Pet. 1:19-21**).

Christ Unlimited — P.O. Box 850 — Dewey, AZ 86327   USA

God: We believe in one God revealed in three persons: the Father, the Son, and the Holy Ghost...making up the blessed Trinity (Matt. 3:16,17; 1 John 5:6,7).

Man: We believe that man, in his natural state, is a sinner —lost, undone, without hope, and without God (Rom. 3:19-23; Gal. 3:22; Eph. 2:1,2,12).

Salvation: We believe the terms of salvation are repentance toward God for sin and a personal, heartfelt faith in the Lord Jesus Christ. This will result in a new birth. Salvation is possible only through God's grace, not by our works. Works are simply the fruit of salvation (Acts 3:19,20; Rom. 4:1-5, 5:1; Eph. 2:8-10).

Body of Christ: We believe the Body of Christ is made up of all who have been born again regardless of denominational differences. We believe in the spirit of unity, while allowing for variety in individual ministries as to their work, calling, and location as directed by the Holy Spirit (Acts 10:34,35; 1 Cor. 12:12-31).

Blood Atonement: We believe in the saving power of the blood of Jesus and His imputed righteousness (Acts 4:12; Rom. 4:1-9, 5:1-11; Eph. 1:3-14).

Bodily Resurrection: We believe in the bodily resurrection of Jesus Christ (Luke 24:39-43; John 20:24-29).

Ascension: We believe that Christ Jesus ascended to the Father and is presently engaged in building a place for us in His Kingdom and interceding for the saints (John 14:2,3; Rom. 8:34).

Second Coming: We believe in the visible, bodily return of Christ Jesus to this earth, to meet His Church (Bride) and to judge the world (Acts 1:10,11; 1 Thess. 4:13-18; 2 Thess. 1:7-10; James 5:8; Rev. 1:7).

Ordinances: We believe that the two ordinances of the Body of Christ are water baptism and the Lord's Supper (Matt. 28:19; 1 Cor.11:24-26).

Heaven and Hell: We believe Scripture clearly sets forth the doctrines of eternal punishment for the lost and eternal bliss and service for the saved — a literal hell for the unsaved and Heaven for the saved (Matt. 25:34,41,46; Luke 16:19-31; John 14:1-3; Rev. 20:11-15).

Holy Spirit: We believe the Holy Spirit to be the third person of the Trinity whose purpose in the redemption of man is to convict of sin, regenerate the repentant believer, guide the believer into all truth, indwell all believers, and give gifts to those He wills that they may minister as Christ would to men. We believe that the manifestations of the Holy Spirit recorded in 1 Corinthians 12:1-11 will operate through present-day Christians who yield to Jesus (Luke 11:13; John 7:37-39, 14:16,17, 16:7-14; Acts 2:1-18).

We believe the baptism in the Holy Spirit, with the evidence of speaking in other tongues as the Spirit gives utterance, is for all believers as promised by John the Baptist (Matt. 3:11), Jesus (Acts 1:4-8), and Peter (Acts 2:38-41). The fulfillment of this promise was witnessed by early disciples of Christ (Acts 2:4, 10:44-47, 19:1-6) and operates in many present-day disciples of the Lord Jesus Christ.

Christ Unlimited — P.O. Box 850 — Dewey, AZ 86327   USA

<u>Divine Healing:</u> We believe God has used doctors, medicines, and other natural means as channels of healing; however, we believe divine healing is provided for believers in the atonement made by Jesus' blood shed on the cross (Isa. 53:5; 1 Pet. 2:24). We believe divine healing may be appropriated by the laying on of hands by the elders (James 5:14-16), by the prayer of an anointed person gifted by the Holy Spirit for healing the sick (1 Cor. 12:9), or by a direct act of receiving this provision by faith (Mark 11:23,24).

MINISTRY FINANCING

> But seek ye first the kingdom of God, and his righteousness; and all these things shall be added unto you.
>
> Matthew 6:33

We want to share with readers the instructions the Lord gave us in regard to financing this ministry. As this is the Holy Spirit's work, we are to let Him speak to the hearts of people as to what and how much He wants them to give. Quite simply, we are to share the vision He has given us and trust Him to provide for all that we need. We believe the Lord pays for the things He orders, and if He does not order something, we do not want to engage in it. Pray with us that we will stay close to the Lord, and that, in seeking His righteousness, we will be able to hear His instructions clearly as to what He desires us to do. If we do that, we know we shall never lack of the things needed to do His work.

CHRIST UNLIMITED MINISTRIES, INC. is a tax-exempt, 501(c)(3) non-profit church, established locally in the Dewey, Arizona area.

[1]Barrett, David B. <u>Cosmos, Chaos, and Gospel</u> (Birmingham: New Hope Publishers, 1987), p. 75.

FOR ADDITIONAL STUDY

This book is taken from a course of Bible studies called the Overcoming Life Series. The entire series is a virtual "spiritual tool chest," as it covers a multitude of subjects every Christian faces in his walk with God. It also answers questions that many believers have concerning the current move of God. These are dealt with in a balanced approach and in the light of the Scripture. God's people are not to live frustrated, defeated lives, but rather they are to be victorious overcomers! Other books available with their companion workbooks are:

PROVE ALL THINGS - Christ warned that great deception would be one of the signs of the end times. In this book, instruction is given on how to recognize false prophets and teachings. Clear Scriptural guidelines are given on discerning the Spirit of truth versus the spirit of error. The book deals with how to judge without being judgmental.

THE TRUE GOD - This is a teaching on the character of God, explaining why God does certain things, and why it is against His nature to do other things. It differentiates between the things for which God is responsible and the things for which the devil is responsible. Our responsibility as Christians destined to overcome is made clear so that we can live victorious lives.

THE WILL OF GOD - This lesson teaches us not only how to know the will of God in our personal lives, family, ministry and finances, but also brings understanding as to why God allows sin, sickness and suffering in the world. As overcomers, Christians are not to suffer under many of the things we have accepted as normal.

KEYS TO THE KINGDOM - Instruction on how to gain authority in God's Kingdom through prayer is the topic of this book. Many principles and methods of prayer are covered, such as praying in the Spirit, fasting and prayer, travailing prayer, praise, intercession and spiritual warfare.

EXPOSING SATAN'S DEVICES - This book is a powerful expose' of Satan's tricks, tactics and lies. Cult and Occultic methods and groups are listed so Christians can detect their activity. Demon activity is discussed and deliverance and casting out demons is dealt with in detail. Satan's kingdom is uncovered and the Christian is taught to overcome through spiritual discernment and warfare.

HEALING OF THE SPIRIT, SOUL AND BODY -This book teaches how to overcome emotional problems, as well as physical ones, and how to receive divine healing. It also teaches how to renew the carnal mind and walk in the spirit of life, thereby overcoming depression, loneliness and fear.

NEITHER MALE NOR FEMALE -What is the woman's role in the church and home? Who is a woman's spiritual head and covering? Does God call women to the five-fold ministry? What does God's Word say about divorce, celibacy and choosing a marriage partner? These and other woman related topics are Scripturally examined.

EXTREMES OR BALANCE? -Many Christians have hurt the cause of Christ through "out-of-balance" teachings and demonstrations. This book shows how to avoid those areas. It also deals wisely with the excesses and extremes in the body of Christ.

THE PATHWAY INTO THE OVERCOMER'S WALK - This book contains answers to the questions an overcomer faces as he presses toward the prize of the high calling in Christ Jesus. How can we be conformed to the image of Christ? How does the Holy Spirit work with the overcomers in the end times? What are the overcomer's rewards?

Please visit our website for information on how to order the complete "Overcoming Life Bible Study." Our site is also an excellent source for additional books and Bible Resources.   www.BibleResources.org

Christ Unlimited — P.O. Box 850 — Dewey, AZ 86327   USA

The Will of God Workbook

Answers to Lessons and Quizzes

Answers to Lesson, Section One

I. Defining God's Will
   A. God's Word is His will.
   B. Logos and Rhema
      1a. Logos — the written Word
      1b. Rhema — the scripture brought to our minds by the Holy Spirit or a word given us through prophecy
      2. Yes, the written and the spoken Word should agree.
      3. No; they cannot disagree and both be right.
      4. Logos

II. How To Find God's Will
   A. 1. The Holy Spirit
      2. The Bible
   B. Yes
   C. 1. "Putting out a fleece"
      2. Asking God to work through circumstances
         a. Gideon
         b. A supernatural sign
   D. The devil can counterfeit signs.

III. Guidelines Given in the Bible
   A. 1. Have a total commitment to God.
      2. Have our minds renewed to the mind of Christ.
      3. Prove or test our decisions by the Word.
      4. Approach God with humility, not pride.
      5. Seek God with a sober mind.
      6. Seek Him in faith.
         a. Dying to self-will and living in the will of God
         b. Those who do not "bear their crosses" (follow Him)
   B. No
      1. Trust, obedience, study, prayer, seeking God
      2. Seeking God with one's whole heart
      3. Pride
      4. When we have our carnal minds renewed from worldly ways so that we have the mind of Christ.

Christ Unlimited — P.O. Box 850 — Dewey, AZ 86327   USA

Answers to Review Outline Quiz, Section One

1. The Word of God and the Holy Spirit
2. John 16:13 and 2 Timothy 3:16,17
3. No, it is not, because man was given the right to make his own choices, and he does not always choose to follow God's will.
4a. Salvation
4b. Healing
5. By faith
6. No, it is not; this is tempting God.
7. Gideon
8. Asking anything according to His will, not our own
9. Knowledge
10. Delighting in His way, His will, and His Word

Christ Unlimited — P.O. Box 850 — Dewey, AZ 86327   USA

Answers to Lesson, Section Two

I.   God's Will for Us in Matters of Health
     A. Healed
        1 "To save" and "To heal"
        2. They choose not to receive.
     B. God wants us to be healed and healthy.
        1. Isaiah 53:5
        2. 1 Peter 2:24

II. God's Will for Us Concerning Suffering
     A.1. Suffering as penalty for sin
        2. Suffering for Christ or for His sake
           a. "bear" and "endure"
           b. Suffering for sin
           c. We have been given authority or power over Satan.
     B.When we obey Him and allow Him to conform us to His image.
        1. Bearing our crosses daily
        2. Staying in difficult circumstances for the sake of those around us;
           fasting to accomplish a spiritual task; leaving comfort to help those in
           discomfort (the lost or hurting); turning the other cheek to injuries and
           not retaliating; losing sleep to pray; enduring accusations without a
           word in return; resisting sin. (Any of these answers, even if not worded
           exactly the same, will show that the principle involved is understood.)
        3. We must choose to suffer for Jesus' sake.
           a. Yes
           b. Yes
     C. Perfect
        1. Suffering
        2. Author — obey

III. Exposing the Lie That Sickness Is God's Will
     A. Job
        1. Satan
        2. Job had his hedge down through sin or his sin was an "open
           door" for satan to enter.
        3. Fear
        4. Self-pity, self-righteousness, pride, and rebellion
        5. No
           a. Eliphaz
           b. Bildad
           c. Zophar
        6. Elihu

Christ Unlimited — P.O. Box 850 — Dewey, AZ 86327   USA

         a. Afflict
         b. Plenty
      7. God Himself
         a. Pride
         b. Creator
      8. By repenting
      9. God restored everything to him and he received a double portion.
   B. Paul
      1. A messenger of Satan (A demon-influenced person who followed Paul, causing persecution and stirring up trouble.)
         a. Because Paul had pride in his life.
         b. Yes
      2. Nations or people who were enemies of Israel and Judah.
      3. In whatever area Paul was weak, he had to depend on God and thus God would get glory by bringing him through victoriously.
         a. Any weakness, lack of strength, or inability to produce results
         b. Sicknesses

IV. God's Way of Chastisement
   A. By His Word and His Spirit
      1. No
      2. To instruct, as in teaching a child
   B. By His Word, in the Bible or His Word through ministers and by the Holy Spirit's conviction of our sins.

V. Consequences of Obedience and Disobedience
   A. 1. Obedience by the things he suffered
       2. Obey
   B. 1. Study the Word.
       2. Keep His commandments.
   C. 1. Destruction in whatever area we are disobedient or ignorant
       2. Shame
       3. We will be devoured by the devil.
       4. The wrath or judgment of God, which is the penalty of sin
          a. Doers
          b. Blessed
   D. Sins, transgressions or wickedness
   E. Evil will come upon us as we reap what we have sown.

Christ Unlimited — P.O. Box 850 — Dewey, AZ 86327   USA

Answers to Review Outline Quiz, Section Two

1. Suffering for Jesus, following His example
2. To choose and receive by faith
3. Totally dying to self
4. Suffering, or denying self, perfects us.
5. Satan, or the devil
6. No, a demon-influenced or possessed person who stirred up trouble for Paul wherever he went
7. They had not yet been perfected of sins of the heart and therefore had " open doors" for the enemy to attack.
8. By His Word and by the Holy Spirit
9. Destruction, shame, reaping in kind what we have sown
10. Psalm 34:19

Christ Unlimited — P.O. Box 850 — Dewey, AZ 86327   USA

www.ingramcontent.com/pod-product-compliance
Lightning Source LLC
Chambersburg PA
CBHW081518040426
42447CB00013B/3264